D...

BR

A MISCELLANY

Compiled by Julia Skinner

With particular reference to the work of Clive Hardy

THE FRANCIS FRITH COLLECTION

www.francisfrith.com

Based on a book first published in the United Kingdom in 2005 by The Francis Frith Collection®

Hardback edition published in 2008 ISBN 978-1-84589-388-0

British Library Cataloguing in Publication Data

Did You Know? Bristol - A Miscellany
Compiled by Julia Skinner
With particular reference to the work of Clive Hardy

The Francis Frith Collection
Frith's Barn, Teffont,
Salisbury, Wiltshire SP3 5QP
Tel: +44 (0) 1722 716 376
Email: info@francisfrith.co.uk
www.francisfrith.com

Printed and bound in Singapore

Front Cover: **BRISTOL, THE BRIDGE 1901** 47883p

The colour-tinting is for illustrative purposes only, and is not intended to be historically accurate

AS WITH ANY HISTORICAL DATABASE, THE FRANCIS FRITH ARCHIVE IS CONSTANTLY BEING CORRECTED AND IMPROVED, AND THE PUBLISHERS WOULD WELCOME INFORMATION ON OMISSIONS OR INACCURACIES

CONTENTS

INTRODUCTION

Bristol was originally known as Bricgstoc (the place of the bridge). Permanent settlement probably began in Anglo-Saxon times around a harbour on the River Avon, developing into a port known as Bristowe by the Middle Ages. By the 12th century there was an established wine trade between Bristol and the Bordeaux region in France, which was later extended to Spain. In the Middle Ages 'Bristowe' became an important trading centre, particularly for the export of wool. In 1552 the Society of Merchant Venturers was founded to extend the city's trade, and Bristol entered its busiest period. Bristol ships and seamen were known in most European ports, and their trade even extended to the Baltic; their efficiency and high standards became a byword - 'all shipshape and Bristol fashion'. Bristol was such a thriving place in the 1660s that it was described by Samuel Pepys as 'in every respect another London'.

Bristol became a major player in the 'triangular trade' between Britain, Africa and the West Indies and America, dealing in wines, tobacco, sugar and chocolate and slaves. Two former household names, Wills tobacco and Fry's chocolate, were Bristol companies. Bristol was heavily involved in the slave trade, and ironically the immigration period of the 1950s, when many West Indians came to live in Britain, would have brought some of the descendants of victims of Bristol's slave trade to settle in the city. In 1990 the late Councillor Jim Williams became Bristol's first black Lord Mayor. In 1999 Pero's Bridge in Bristol was opened as a memorial to those who suffered as a result of the trade, and in recognition of the part they played in the wealth of Bristol in the past.

Did You Know?
BRISTOL
A MISCELLANY

Bristol declined as a port in the 19th century, as a result of a combination of high dock charges, the silting up of the River Avon and competition from Liverpool. However its 19th-century history is noteworthy for the work of Isambard Kingdom Brunel, who not only had his famous ships, the 'Great Western' (1837) and the 'Great Britain' (1843), built and launched at Bristol, but also designed the Clifton Suspension Bridge, one of the most famous city landmarks, although he did not live to see it completed.

Bristol suffered considerable bomb damage during the Second World War, but the city landscape still has fine churches, and Georgian and Regency crescents and terraces that were built by prosperous merchants. Bristol's past is full of fascinating characters, events and stories, of which this book can only give a brief glimpse.

BRISTOL, QUEENS ROAD 1900 45653a

BRISTOL DIALECT WORDS AND SAYINGS

'Brizzle' - a jocular pronunciation for Bristol.

'Gert' - great, good.

'Bemmie' - the Bedminster area.

'Where's that to?' - where is it?

'Keener' - a hard worker.

'Ow bist?' - how are you?

'Pay on the nail' - The brass pillars, or nails, in Corn Street, outside what used to be the Bristol Exchange, were used by merchants when striking a bargain. The money was paid on the nail head, hence the phrase 'pay on the nail' (see page 45).

'All Shipshape and Bristol Fashion' - means that everything has been stowed and the ship is in every way ready for the sea. The phrase thus means that all is completely organised and ready. It derives from the port of Bristol's reputation for efficiency in the days of sail.

HAUNTED BRISTOL

All Saints' Church is reputedly haunted by the ghost of a monk who hid the church's treasures from Henry VIII's officers at the time of the Dissolution, and returns to guard their hiding place - the treasures were never found.

When the new Fire Brigade Headquarters in Temple Back was built in 1975, there were at least nine reported sightings of a ghost which walked through closed doors, and apparently caused the temperature to drop. One lady saw the ghost three times, and described it as a man in his thirties, wearing what she thought was a long coat. As the Temple area of Bristol was once owned by the medieval order of warrior monks called the Knights Templar, one theory suggests that the site was haunted by the ghost of one of these knights, in a medieval robe, checking out the development.

Pembroke Road is haunted by the ghost of Jenkins Protheroe, a dwarf highwayman who was hanged there in 1783.

> The Black Castle, a pub at St Philip's Causeway, Brislington, boasts two ghosts, of a young girl and a nun. That of the nun is most often reported, although her spirit is felt as a presence rather than seen as an apparition, and she is believed to emanate from a little chapel at the top of one of the towers of the building.

A house in Air Balloon Road in the St George's area was apparently haunted by four ghosts in recent times. The ghosts were identified by a medium as a boy called Tom, a woman in an old-fashioned black dress, a man called David and a youth called Peter. The owners of the house also reported that old coins appeared from nowhere, footsteps were heard, and the family dog appeared distressed in certain parts of the house. The owners enlisted the help of the Bristol Evening Post in 1998 to try to find out the stories behind the hauntings.

BRISTOL MISCELLANY

On either side of St John's Gate are the figures of Brennus and Belinus, legendary founders of Bristol.

After 1552, when Bristol's Merchant Venturers were incorporated, sea-going Bristol ships could be found anywhere in the known world. Though most were involved in the trade with Spain, during the 1580s several Bristol ships made trips to the Baltic.

Bristol had a turbulent Civil War. It was of vital strategic importance to both Royalist and Parliamentary sides, and was in the possession of both at various times during the war. It could be argued that the king's cause, and the war, was lost when Prince Rupert finally surrendered Bristol to Parliament on 10 September 1645.

During the 18th century a large number of Bristol vessels undertook voyages as privateers; sailing under letters of marque, a privateer was a privately-owned vessel authorised to wage war upon the king's enemies in exchange for prize money. During the American War of Independence (1776-83), 157 Bristol ships sailed under letters of marque, and during the French Revolution and the Napoleonic Wars, from 1793 to 1815, the city furnished a total of 63 privateers.

Elizabeth Blackwell (1821-1910) was born in Bristol, the daughter of a sugar refiner. After emigrating to the USA with her family and studying medicine in Geneva, she eventually moved to London, where she became the first woman to enrol with the British Medical Register. She died in Bristol in 1910.

BRISTOL, THE ENTRANCE TO THE DOCKS 1900 45555

CLIFTON, THE SUSPENSION BRIDGE 1887 20164

In 1828 Isambard Kingdom Brunel was staying at Clifton for the good of his health, spending much of his time on sketching expeditions along the Clifton Gorge. By coincidence, in October 1829 the Merchant Venturers advertised plans to bridge the Gorge, since money had been left for the purpose by William Vick in 1752. Despite competition from experienced engineers such as Thomas Telford, one of young Isambard's sketches was selected. Brunel's original estimate had been £52,966, but by the time the final design was ready the price had gone up to £57,000. Vick's legacy would not now be enough, and it would be August 1836 before the foundation stone was laid. The bridge was not finally completed until 1864, after Brunel's death. At 245 feet above the Avon Gorge, it has attracted many suicides and, lately, bungee jumpers.

Despite Bristol's reputation as a slaving city, not all the slaves handled by Bristol were from Africa. From the early years of the 17th century thousands of men and women were sentenced by English courts to servitude in the colonies of the New World, many destined to leave from the port of Bristol to work on sugar plantations in the West Indies.

Because it lacks a clerestory and triforium, the aisles of Bristol Cathedral rise to the same height as the nave, a feature making Bristol unique among English cathedrals.

BRISTOL, THE CATHEDRAL 1887 20141

BRISTOL, THE BRIDGE AND THE CHURCH OF ST NICHOLAS 1901 47883

Bishop Secker's Diocese Book has an interesting comment on members of the congregation of the church of St Nicholas: Abel Edwards was a profane swearer, blasphemer and drunkard, John Veal lived in sin with Deborah Orstand, and Thomas Williams and George Barrat appear to have kept bawdy houses. The clock on St Nicholas's Church is the only public clock in England with a second hand.

BRISTOL, THE VIEW FROM THE GRANARY 1901 47880

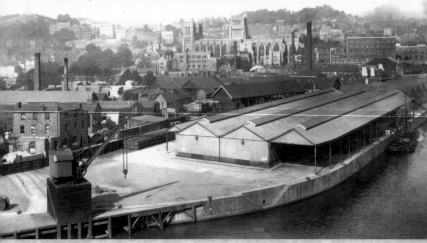

The development of Avonmouth helped to bring back some shipping to Bristol in the 20th century. From 1921 liners from Rangoon in Burma and Colombo in Ceylon (now Sri Lanka) were making scheduled calls at Avonmouth. In 1901 Elder & Fyffe inaugurated their fortnightly service to Port Limon, Costa Rica. For over 60 years the banana ships would use Avonmouth, which involved the railways in operating over 400 special banana trains a year. Between 1922-23 the eastern arm of the Royal Edward dock was built, alongside which were constructed large transit sheds and granaries. In 1938 the docks handled 51 ships, carrying 231,000 tons of fruit, oilseeds, rice and tea from India, Burma, Ceylon and Malaya, while a further 86 ships discharged over 200,000 tons of cargo from Australia and New Zealand. The total for that year was 354 ships, with more than one million tons of cargo landed.

It is estimated that in the mid 19th century over 200 horse-drawn coaches arrived and departed daily from the various inns in Bristol, such as the White Hart and the Bush.

As well as being a large, prosperous city and port, Bristol, or more accurately Clifton, developed as a spa. The Hotwells proved popular with high society, especially after the discovery of a second spa in 1702. During the 18th century Clifton became a fashionable resort, in that part of the country second only to Bath. The resort had all the amenities one would expect; a pump room and assembly rooms were built in 1722, and some London shops would even open branches there for the season.

CLIFTON FROM THE DOWNS 1896 38165

Slavery became Bristol's main traffic in the early 18th century. In 1725, for example, 63 ships cleared Bristol to take part in the slave trade along the West African coast, with a total capacity for 16,950 slaves. Although Bristol and London controlled slaving in the early 18th century, they were soon to be eclipsed by a new player, Liverpool. With a different pay structure in operation, Liverpool ships were more profitable per voyage. Between 1756 and 1786 a total of 588 slaving voyages were made from Bristol, while Liverpool vessels made 1,858. However the slavers did not always have things their own way. In May 1750 the Bristol slaver 'King David' was overrun by slaves who had managed to break into the arms locker. The captain and five crewmen were killed, while the rest of the crew took refuge in the hold. The leader of the slaves, who spoke good English, told the surviving crewmen that if they came up on deck they would be spared, but as each man came topside he was put in irons and thrown overboard. The mate was the last to come up, and was only spared when it was realised that there was no-one else left who knew how to handle the ship or navigate.

Every year in August the skies above Bristol are filled with hot-air balloons, as Bristol hosts an International Balloon Fiesta at Ashton Court, the largest balloon fiesta in Europe. Up to 100 balloons are launched at a time, in a wide variety of shapes and colours.

It was at the top of Christmas Steps (see page 15) that John Foster founded an almshouse and chapel in 1481. The chapel, which was heavily restored in the 1880s, has an unusual dedication to the Three Kings of Cologne, probably because John Foster traded with Cologne, and may have copied this dedication from Cologne Cathedral.

BRISTOL, CHRISTMAS STEPS c1950 B212263

BRISTOL, THE DOCKS c1950 B212220

The railway came to Bristol in 1835 with the opening of the southern section of the Bristol & Gloucester Railway, which involved the construction of the 515-yards-long Staple Hill Tunnel. The Bristol terminus was at Avonside Wharf on the Floating Harbour. The second railway to enter the city was the Great Western Railway, whose first train ran on the Bristol to Bath section on 31 August 1840. Ten trains operated on the first day, carrying nearly 6,000 passengers. The third railway to come to Bristol was the Bristol & Exeter, with twelve Bristolians on the sixteen-strong board of directors, and Isambard Kingdom Brunel appointed as an engineer. The line was worked with GWR locomotives and rolling stock, and when it opened throughout, in May 1844, it was the longest main line in the country: the distance between London and Exeter was 194 miles.

Did You Know?
BRISTOL
A MISCELLANY

The chains used to support the Clifton suspension bridge were bought secondhand, having been used on the old Hungerford Bridge in London.

Originally Bristol's College Green was the burial ground for the Augustinian abbey founded by Robert Fitzharding in 1148, and for a hospital, founded jointly by Maurice Berkely of Gaunt and his nephew Robert de Gourey.

Medieval Bristol had two hospitals for lepers: St Mary Magdalene's, Brightbow, was for women, while a similar institution for men existed to the east of the town boundary.

CLIFTON, THE SUSPENSION BRIDGE 1887 20168

St Augustine's Reach dates from the 13th century and used to extend the river further into the town. When it was built in 1248 it was an outstanding piece of civil engineering for its time, as it

involved the diverting of the River Avon from its junction with the Avon at Bristol Bridge. The Reach established Bristol as the major port on the west coast at that time.

BRISTOL, A VIEW FROM THE CENTRE TOWARDS ST AUGUSTINE'S REACH c1950 B212266

BRISTOL, THE STATUE OF JOHN CABOT 2005 B212712 (Courtesy of Matthew Skinner)

Isambard Kingdom Brunel's steamships, 'Great Western' and 'Great Britain', were built at Bristol, although both were too big to be able to use the Floating Harbour. The 'Great Western', which pioneered transatlantic steamer services, was a wooden paddle-steamer of 1,340 tons, and although she was based at Kingroad, near the mouth of the Avon, the money-grabbing Bristol Dock Co still demanded full port dues on her. The 'Great Britain', being a much larger vessel and built of iron, was immediately based at Liverpool, where she was joined by the 'Great Western' in 1842. Both ships drew large crowds when they were first towed out of Bristol and through the Gorge at Clifton. The 'Great Britain' has now returned to Bristol and has been restored, drawing thousands of visitors each year.

In 1497 John Cabot set sail from Bristol in search of lands to the west, looking for new markets and fishing grounds to extend Bristol's trade. He discovered mainland north America, and the following year his son Sebastian explored the American coast from Newfoundland to Florida. The new continent the Cabots reached may actually have been named after their patron, the Bristol merchant Richard Amerycke. A replica of John Cabot's tiny ship, the 'Matthew', was sailed to Newfoundland in 1999 to commemorate the voyages of the Cabots, and can now be seen at Bristol's Great Western dock.

When the side-saddle traveller Celia Fiennes visited Bristol in 1698 she commented 'the streetes are well pitch'd and preserved by their using sleds to carry all things about'. The sleds were used in preference to wheeled traffic so as not to disturb Bristol's system of underground sewers, a much-admired rarity in the late 17th century.

The church of St Mary Redcliffe houses some interesting artefacts, including what is purported to be a rib from the Dun Cow said to have been slain by Guy of Warwick; it is in fact a whalebone, thought to have been presented by John Cabot. In front of the high altar of St Mary Redcliffe is a brass to John Brooke and his wife Johanna. She was the daughter of Richard Amerycke, collector for customs and patron of John Cabot.

For centuries a major problem facing the Bristol Health Board was how to combat the daily stench during the summer months created by tons of horse droppings. An early experiment using water carts to damp down the streets found that it took 7,000 gallons to water one mile of street. The result of this 1861 experiment found that Bristol would need 83 carts to water the streets twice a day.

Bristol's electric tramway system was inaugurated on 14 October 1895. The tramway was operated by a private company, rather than the Corporation, until 1937. The Tramways Act of 1870 gave powers to Bristol Corporation to take over the system at book price in 1915, or at any seventh year thereafter. Every seven years the council could not decide to make a firm commitment. The result was that the tramway company spent very little on upgrading the system, and it remained virtually unaltered throughout its 46-year existence. The Bristol Tramways & Carriage Co was eventually taken over by the Corporation in 1937. All 237 trams were identical and all were open-topped. The tramway closed in April 1941 when a bomb destroyed the power supply.

BRISTOL, THE UNIVERSITY FROM CABOT TOWER c1950 B212203

When Celia Fiennes visited Bristol in 1698 she noted that there were nineteen parish churches. However there was no official place of worship for Catholics until the 1730s, and even then this was only created out of necessity. Abraham Darby owned a brass works in the city, but in order to beat off foreign competition he needed to employ skilled Flemish workers; they would only come to Bristol if they were allowed to worship freely as Catholics.

Edmund Blanket was a 14th-century Bristol resident who is traditionally believed to have invented the blanket. He is buried in St Stephen's Church.

The church of St Mary Redcliffe is as large as a cathedral, and is one of only two parish churches in England to have stone vaulting. St Mary's was built on a large scale thanks to the generosity of Bristol merchants. The name Redcliffe derives from the red sandstone outcrop upon which St Mary's stands. The church itself is built of oolitic limestone. The church was visited by Queen Elizabeth I in 1574, who described it as the 'fairest and goodliest' church in England, although she was less impressed with the Bristol women - 'Good Lord master Mayor, how plain the women of Bristol be!'

BRISTOL, ST MARY REDCLIFFE 1887 20153

To the left of this photograph is one of the cone-shaped furnaces of a glassworks. In 1793 Bristol had at least a dozen glassworks, producing a wide variety of glass and bottles for customers throughout the West Country.

BRISTOL 1900 45563

After the Monmouth Rebellion of 1685, Judge Jeffreys held one of his Bloody Assizes in the old Bristol Guildhall. The Bristol rebels were called 'mere sons of dunghills' by the judge, who sentenced six of them to be hanged.

In 1801-02 the engineer William Jessop came up with his own designs for a tide-free city dock area that would enclose the Avon from Rownham to St Philip's. The river itself would be diverted by means of a New Cut from Totterdown to the entrance of the Floating Harbour. The project was completed by 1809, at a cost of about £600,000, with French prisoners of war being used for much of the manual labour.

In 1823 the Chamber of Commerce were so concerned about the high cost of the port dues being demanded by the Bristol Dock Co that they enquired as to what charges would be levied at other ports for the same cargo. At Bristol the dues would be £515,608, at Liverpool £231,800, at London £210,098, and at Hull £147,587. By the mid 1840s it was cheaper to discharge goods at Liverpool, and then transport them by rail to Bristol, that it was to discharge them at the Bristol docks, which was partly the reason for the decline of Bristol's trade.

Bristol has its own leaning tower, at Temple Church, which has leaned at this precarious angle since the 14th century.

In the churchyard of St Mary Redcliffe is a memorial to 'The Church Cat', who used to sit on the organist's lap and listen to the music.

Opened in 1836 by the Bristol General Cemetery Co, Arnos Vale became the city's main burial ground until augmented by the opening of Greenbank Cemetery during the 1870s. Arnos Vale was laid out in terraces and Charles Underwood designed its Doric lodges and classical chapels. The cemetery was featured in the BBC 'Restoration' series.

The history of chocolate-making in the Bristol area goes back to the middle of the 18th century when the physician Dr Joseph Fry began to make chocolate at his apothecary shop. At that time chocolate was used either as a drink or mixed with medicine to make it more palatable. Dr Fry was a Quaker, and the manufacture of chocolate was especially important to him as it was a temperance drink. In 1793 Dr Fry's son, Joseph Storrs Fry, moved the chocolate-making business to premises in Union Street. J S Fry & Sons Ltd merged with Cadbury in the 20th century, and chocolate and confectionery has been made on the Cadbury Somerdale site in Keynsham since the 1930s. Many chocolate favourites are made at Somerdale, including Crunchie, Picnic and Fry's Turkish Delight.

Blackbeard the Pirate was a Bristol man, real name either Edward Drummond or Edward Teach.

St Werburgh's Church formerly stood in Corn Street. An interesting gravestone in its churchyard read:

'Here lies a Brown - a White - the colours one
Pale drawn by death, here shaded by a stone
One house did hold them both while life did last
One grave do hold them both, now life is past.'

The couple were Humphrey Brown, a merchant who died in 1630, and his wife Elizabeth, whose maiden name was White.

BRISTOL, OLD HOUSES AND TOLLEY'S BANK 1890 24641

BRISTOL, COLLEGE GREEN 1887 20128

The Red Maids School was founded by John Whitston, who died in 1629. Once a year he is remembered by the pupils when they hold a candlelit service in front of his effigy in the crypt of St Nicholas's Church on St Nicholas Street.

The Llandoger Trow, an old inn in King Street, was once the drinking den of pirates and is believed to have been the inspiration for the Admiral Benbow pub in Robert Louis Stevenson's 'Treasure Island'. The Hole in the Wall in Queen Square is reputedly the original for the Spyglass in the same book.

The 16-feet-high statue of Nelson on his column in London's Trafalgar Square was carved by a Bristol man, Edward Hodges Baily.

Samuel Plimsoll was born in Redcliffe in 1824. He campaigned for safer conditions at sea, which led to the passing of the Merchant Shipping Act in 1876.

Pero's Bridge was built in 1999, and is named after Pero, who lived approx 1753-1798 and was the slave of a rich Bristol merchant called John Pinney. The bridge was so-named to commemorate the contribution of black people to the development of the city, and their importance to the economy of Bristol in the past, as well as an acknowledgement of the suffering caused by slavery.

BRISTOL, PERO'S BRIDGE 2005 B212721 (Courtesy of Matthew Skinner)

In the early days of sail, vessels making their way up the Avon to Bristol had to contend with several problems: the current, the wind through the Gorge, and the serpentine course of the river itself.

Vessels were assisted by towboats, usually manned by ten or more rowers, and depending on the size of the ship and the prevailing conditions anything up to ten rowboats might be needed.

BRISTOL, THE HARBOUR c1950 B212181

BRISTOL, THE THEATRE ROYAL 1890 24640

Bristol's Theatre Royal, built in 1766, is the oldest existing theatre in England. It is believed to be haunted by two ghosts, one of which moves items around in the theatre's paint shop.

The Queen Victoria Fountain in St Nicholas Street was erected in 1859 to mark Queen Victoria's 40th birthday.

In the choir of Bristol Cathedral is a stained glass window which is said to have been donated by Charles II's mistress Nell Gwynn, in thanks for her safe recovery from an illness.

The Edward Everard Building in Broad Street, built in 1900-01 to house a printing works, is a triumph of Art Nouveau design; the ceramic façade was the work of W J Neatby, head of the architectural department at Doulton's. A life-sized ceramic figure of Gutenburg - the father of printing - works at his press surrounded by his 1490s alphabet. Facing him is William Morris who revived the craft, surrounded by his 1890s alphabet. The spirit of literature touches the tips of both presses with her wings and the figure holding a mirror and lamp presides, symbolising light and truth. When the building was unveiled it caused a sensation, and the police were called into control the crowds.

BRISTOL, THE CENTRE 1953 B212283

Bristol Milk and Bristol Cream are two sherries which are world famous. Fuller, in his 'History of the Worthies of England', wrote 'though as many elephants are fed as cows grazed within the walls of this city, yet great plenty of this Metaphorical Milk,

BRISTOL, PARK STREET 1900 45653

whereby Xeres or Sherry-sack is intended, is consumed...'. This
'Metaphorical Milk' inspired Edward VII's famous phrase:
'All I can say is you've got fine cows!'

SPORTING BRISTOL

James Peters, who played for Bristol Rugby Club, holds the distinction of being the first black player to represent England. An outside-half, he played 35 times for Bristol from 1900-02. He made the first of his five England appearances in 1906, whilst a Plymouth player. He played his last game for England at Ashton Gate in Bristol.

Surely the greatest Bristol-born figure in sporting history was the legendary cricketer W G Grace, who was born in 1848 in Downend. A few statistics tell a great deal about him: he played for 44 seasons, scored 54,000 runs, and took 2,800 wickets. As a qualified doctor, he once had to treat an opponent who was impaled on a fence! In his day he was also thought to be the best-known Englishman other than Mr Gladstone, the Prime Minister. W G Grace is generally thought of as cricket's first 'superstar', and he is thought to have earned a modern-day equivalent of £1-million from the game.

The well-known song 'Goodnight Irene' is the favourite song sung by Bristol Rovers supporters. It was apparently regularly sung as pre-match entertainment at Eastville stadium by the Five Smith Brothers. Rovers fans identified with one particular line, 'Sometimes I have a great notion, to jump in the river and drown', especially when Rovers lost; the Bristol Frome ran alongside the ground, so it was particularly appropriate!

In the 2002-03 season, Bristol City's forwards had an incredible season. They scored 106 goals, a huge total, but they still failed to gain promotion from Division Two; they missed out by three points, and then lost in the play-offs.

Did You Know?
BRISTOL
A MISCELLANY

QUIZ QUESTIONS

Answers on page 49.

1. What was the rather unpleasant hobby of Richard Smith, chief surgeon at Bristol's Royal Infirmary in the 19th century?

2. Which major military figure of the First World War spent his schooldays in Bristol?

3. What is Bristol's link between education, cigarettes and the performing arts?

4. How many places in North America share Bristol's name?

5. Which famous Hollywood star was Bristol-born?

6. What unfortunate accident befell 14-year-old Henry Hallard in Frogmore Street in 1864?

7. Which famous authoress was married at Emmanuel Church, Clifton, in 1914?

8. What is the link between Bristol and a certain cheese-loving animated character and his long-suffering dog?

9. Which Bristol-born poet coined the phrase 'Curses are like young chickens, they always come home to roost'?

10. What is the link between Bristol Cathedral and Robinson Crusoe?

BRISTOL, THE CABOT TOWER 1900 45564

RECIPE

TREACLE BREAD

One of the main imports into Bristol from the West Indies was sugar.
Sugar is used to make black treacle.

Ingredients:

4oz/115g Black Treacle (ie
Fowler's West India Treacle)
2 eggs, well beaten
1 level teaspoon EACH of
cinnamon and mixed spice
Half a level teaspoon
bicarbonate of soda

2oz/50g EACH of currants
and sultanas
Quarter pint/125ml milk
10oz/275g plain flour
Half a level teaspoon baking
powder
2oz/50g butter or margarine

Combine treacle and milk, then add beaten eggs.

Sift dry ingredients, rub in fat, add fruit and mix to a soft consistency
with the liquid.

Turn into a well-greased 2lb/1kg loaf tin and bake in the centre of
a slow oven, Gas Mark 3 or 160 degrees C/325 degrees F for 1 to
1¾ hours. Turn out on to a wire tray, slice when cold and serve with
butter.

BRISTOL, ONE OF THE PILLARS ('NAILS') OUTSIDE THE CORN EXCHANGE, CORN STREET 2005 B212708 (Courtesy of Matthew Skinner)

BRISTOL, CORN EXCHANGE, CORN STREET 2005
B212701 (Courtesy of Matthew Skinner)

RECIPE

The suburb of Clifton is known for its Regency crescents and Georgian terraces. Royal York Crescent, overlooking the Gorge, is the largest crescent in England.

CLIFTON PUFFS
A traditional small cake, which is rich yet light.

Ingredients:

I packet frozen puff pastry - or make your own if preferred.

Filling ingredients -

8 oz/225g (1cup) peeled, cored and finely chopped eating apples

8 oz/225g (1 cup) currants

4 oz/115g (half cup) seedless raisins

8oz/225g (1 cup) chopped candied peel

16oz/450g (2 cups) blanched chopped almonds

Half a teaspoon grated nutmeg

4-6 tablespoons brandy

Defrost puff pastry.

Mix all the filling ingredients well, cover and leave in a warm place to infuse for about one hour. Then roll out the pastry very thinly and cut into 4-in squares. Put some of the mixture on one half of each square, damp the edges and fold over cornerwise, making triangles. Brush with beaten egg, dust with coarsely crushed sugar and bake in a hot oven (400 degrees F, Gas Mark 6, 200 degrees C) for about 15-20 minutes, or until the pastry is risen and a pale gold. They are best served warm.

Makes about 20.

QUIZ ANSWERS

1. Richard Smith, chief surgeon at the Royal Infirmary and a councillor from 1835 to 1842, was one of Bristol's flamboyant characters. His hobby was to write a rhyme relating to the career of every local criminal who had been executed and then sent to him for dissection (in the early days of surgery this was the only legal way by which surgeons and students could obtain bodies for the study of anatomy). Smith would then bind the pages in the skin of the unfortunate felon.

2. Douglas Haig (1861-1928), who became Commander-in-Chief of the British Army in France during the First World War, and who planned the Somme offensive, was a Clifton College Old Boy.

3. Incorporated in 1909, the main buildings of Bristol University, in Park Street, were paid for by Sir George Arthur Wills and his brother Henry Herbert Wills (of the tobacco family) in memory of their father. The Tobacco Factory on Raleigh Road, Southville, is the last remaining part of the old Wills Tobacco site. It now houses a restaurant, a bar and offices, apartments, and an excellent performing arts studio.

4. There are at least 28 places called Bristol in the USA, and 4 in Canada.

5. The Hollywood star Cary Grant was originally from Bristol - however his real name was Archibald Leach!

6. He was 'knocked down by a lady's crinoline', and suffered a fractured leg.

7. Agatha Miller married Captain Archibald Christie in 1914 at Emmanuel Church, Clifton. Although the marriage did not last, she became famous as the authoress Agatha Christie.

8. Bristol is the home of Aardman Animations and Nick Park, creators of Wallace and Gromit.

9. The poet Robert Southey, who was born in Wine Street in 1774. This phrase comes from 'The Curse of Kehama'.

10. In Bristol Cathedral are some candlesticks which were thanksgiving gifts from the privateers who rescued Alexander Selkirk from a desert island in 1709. Captain Woodes Rogers, who lived at 33-35 Queen Square, brought Selkirk to Bristol. Daniel Defoe was inspired by Selkirk's story, and used it as the basis of his novel 'Robinson Crusoe'.

CLIFTON, THE DOWNS HOTEL 1887 20182

FRANCIS FRITH

PIONEER VICTORIAN PHOTOGRAPHER

Francis Frith, founder of the world-famous photographic archive, was a complex and multi-talented man. A devout Quaker and a highly successful Victorian businessman, he was philosophical by nature and pioneering in outlook. By 1855 he had already established a wholesale grocery business in Liverpool, and sold it for the astonishing sum of £200,000, which is the equivalent today of over £15,000,000. Now in his thirties, and captivated by the new science of photography, Frith set out on a series of pioneering journeys up the Nile and to the Near East.

INTRIGUE AND EXPLORATION

He was the first photographer to venture beyond the sixth cataract of the Nile. Africa was still the mysterious 'Dark Continent', and Stanley and Livingstone's historic meeting was a decade into the future. The conditions for picture taking confound belief. He laboured for hours in his wicker dark-room in the sweltering heat of the desert, while the volatile chemicals fizzed dangerously in their trays. Back in London he exhibited his photographs and was 'rapturously cheered' by members of the Royal Society. His reputation as a photographer was made overnight.

VENTURE OF A LIFE-TIME

By the 1870s the railways had threaded their way across the country, and Bank Holidays and half-day Saturdays had been made obligatory by Act of Parliament. All of a sudden the working man and his family were able to enjoy days out, take holidays, and see a little more of the world.

With typical business acumen, Francis Frith foresaw that these new tourists would enjoy having souvenirs to commemorate their days out. For the next thirty years he travelled the country by train and by pony and trap, producing fine photographs of seaside resorts and beauty spots that were keenly bought by millions of Victorians. These prints were painstakingly pasted into family albums and pored over during the dark nights of winter, rekindling precious memories of summer excursions. Frith's studio was soon supplying retail shops all over the country, and by 1890 F Frith & Co had become the greatest specialist photographic publishing company in the world, with over 2,000 sales outlets, and pioneered the picture postcard.

FRANCIS FRITH'S LEGACY

Francis Frith had died in 1898 at his villa in Cannes, his great project still growing. By 1970 the archive he created contained over a third of a million pictures showing 7,000 British towns and villages.

Frith's legacy to us today is of immense significance and value, for the magnificent archive of evocative photographs he created provides a unique record of change in the cities, towns and villages throughout Britain over a century and more. Frith and his fellow studio photographers revisited locations many times down the years to update their views, compiling for us an enthralling and colourful pageant of British life and character.

We are fortunate that Frith was dedicated to recording the minutiae of everyday life. For it is this sheer wealth of visual data, the painstaking chronicle of changes in dress, transport, street layouts, buildings, housing and landscape that captivates us so much today, offering us a powerful link with the past and with the lives of our ancestors.

Computers have now made it possible for Frith's many thousands of images to be accessed almost instantly. The archive offers every one of us an opportunity to examine the places where we and our families have lived and worked down the years. Its images, depicting our shared past, are now bringing pleasure and enlightenment to millions around the world a century and more after his death.

For further information visit: www.francisfrith.com

INTERIOR DECORATION

Frith's photographs can be seen framed and as giant wall murals in thousands of pubs, restaurants, hotels, banks, retail stores and other public buildings throughout Britain. These provide interesting and attractive décor, generating strong local interest and acting as a powerful reminder of gentler days in our increasingly busy and frenetic world.

FRITH PRODUCTS

All Frith photographs are available as prints and posters in a variety of different sizes and styles. In the UK we also offer a range of other gift and stationery products illustrated with Frith photographs, although many of these are not available for delivery outside the UK – see our web site for more information on the products available for delivery in your country.

THE INTERNET

Over 100,000 photographs of Britain can be viewed and purchased on the Frith web site. The web site also includes memories and reminiscences contributed by our customers, who have personal knowledge of localities and of the people and properties depicted in Frith photographs. If you wish to learn more about a specific town or village you may find these reminiscences fascinating to browse. Why not add your own comments if you think they would be of interest to others? See **www.francisfrith.com**

PLEASE HELP US BRING FRITH'S PHOTOGRAPHS TO LIFE

Our authors do their best to recount the history of the places they write about. They give insights into how particular towns and villages developed, they describe the architecture of streets and buildings, and they discuss the lives of famous people who lived there. But however knowledgeable our authors are, the story they tell is necessarily incomplete.

Frith's photographs are so much more than plain historical documents. They are living proofs of the flow of human life down the generations. They show real people at real moments in history; and each of those people is the son or daughter of someone, the brother or sister, aunt or uncle, grandfather or grandmother of someone else. All of them lived, worked and played in the streets depicted in Frith's photographs.

We would be grateful if you would give us your insights into the places shown in our photographs: the streets and buildings, the shops, businesses and industries. Post your memories of life in those streets on the Frith website: what it was like growing up there, who ran the local shop and what shopping was like years ago; if your workplace is shown tell us about your working day and what the building is used for now. Read other visitors' memories and reconnect with your shared local history and heritage. With your help more and more Frith photographs can be brought to life, and vital memories preserved for posterity, and for the benefit of historians in the future.

Wherever possible, we will try to include some of your comments in future editions of our books. Moreover, if you spot errors in dates, titles or other facts, please let us know, because our archive records are not always completely accurate—they rely on 140 years of human endeavour and hand-compiled records. You can email us using the contact form on the website.

Thank you!

For further information, trade, or author enquiries
please contact us at the address below:

**The Francis Frith Collection, Frith's Barn, Teffont,
Salisbury, Wiltshire, England SP3 5QP.**

Tel: +44 (0)1722 716 376 Fax: +44 (0)1722 716 881
e-mail: sales@francisfrith.co.uk **www.francisfrith.com**